THE
KEY
OF ABRAHAM

THE BLESSING
OR THE CURSE

DOMINIQUAE
BIERMAN, PHD

Published by Zion's Gospel Press

52 Tuscan Way, Ste 202-412
St. Augustine, FL, 32092
shalom@zionsgospel.com

Paperback ISBN: 978-1-953502-49-0
E-Book ISBN: 978-1-953502-50-6

On occasion words such as Jesus, Christ, Lord and God have been changed by the author, back to their original Hebrew renderings, Yeshua, Messiah, Yahveh, and Elohim.

Bold or italicized emphasis or underlining within quotations is the author's own.

Printed in the United States of America

First Printing April 2009, Second Printing April 2011, June 2021

Acknowledgments & Thanksgiving

To my heavenly Father who has given me this incredible mandate and the grace to obey it. To my husband, Baruch, who "puts me on the spot" every time I want to pull back. Without his encouragement, I would have not dared to publish this daring book! To my EA and secretary, Karen, who is an amazing woman of many talents and much faithfulness. She helps keep me "together" when there is too much on my plate. and is a true daughter! To Paul and Marilyn Hueper from Homer, Alaska, that provided an awesome "room with a view" for me to write this book in; and to Marilyn for proofreading it. To all those, throughout the nations, that have believed in my calling and have supported me financially, in prayer and in friendship. May THE KEY OF ABRAHAM be in the blessing position for you forever!

"I will bless those that bless you."
—Genesis 12:3a

Yours in Messiah,
Archbishop Dr. Dominiquae Bierman

IMPORTANT PROPHETIC INSIGHT

This book was written in Homer, Alaska, in 2004 and was published in Eilat, Israel, in 2009. It was written in the cold North of the World MAP and it was published in the hot South Gate of Israel, Eilat, on the Red Sea. This in itself is a prophetic statement on the importance of this message that needs to cover the world map!

> *"The Mighty One God, YAHVEH, has spoken, and summoned the earth from the rising of the sun to its setting. Out of Zion, the perfection of beauty, God has shone forth."*
> —Psalms 50:1-2

CONTENTS

INTRODUCTION
RESTORED TERMINOLOGY

I want to introduce a few terms that I will use throughout the entire book with no further explanation:

Yahveh

Yahveh is the name of the LORD as revealed to Moses and used throughout the prophetic writings. It means "The I AM and the Ever Present God."

This name is often used in conjunction with the name *ELOHIM*, which is the name of the Creator God.

Elohim

The name of the LORD when He is revealing Himself as the Creator. Yahveh ELOHIM, "The I AM who is The Creator"

In the beginning ELOHIM created the heavens and the earth.
—Genesis 1:1

Yah

Translated as God. Yah as in HalleluYah. So, many times I will use the Word Yah instead of the Word God.

Extol Him that rideth upon the heavens by His name Yah.

—Psalm 68:4

The Torah

Torah is the Hebrew word for "instruction in righteousness," commonly called Law. In this book Torah only refers to the Law of Yahveh in the five books of Moses and throughout the Bible.

In this book, Torah does not refer to any rabbinical Laws or man-made traditions. In a place where I mention a rabbinical tradition, I will refer to it as such.

Because Abraham obeyed my voice, and kept my charge, my Commandments, my statutes and my Laws (Torah).

—Genesis 26:5

Please note that even prior to the giving of the Torah at Mount Sinai, Abraham already walked and obeyed it, because the Torah of the Living Yah is eternal.

Important: the Torah includes three types of Laws:

- Commandments
- Statutes or Judgments
- Laws or Precepts

The Commandments, i.e., the Ten Commandments, are forever.

The statutes are also forever, and they are connected with holiness and Worship. Following the statutes that are connected with Temple worship requires more knowledge of their background and a Holy Spirit interpretation. This is necessary in order to learn and know how to follow them today through the Spirit who gives life, since we are now the Temple of the Holy Spirit.

The precepts are eternal principles that are relevant and directed to the issues of the time in which they were given, although the actual instructions were temporary. So today we keep the principles and apply it to our times. As we walk with the Holy Spirit of Yah, He continues to give us precepts daily.

The ticket to success and prosperity in life:

This Book of the Law (Torah) shall not depart from your mouth, but you shall meditate on it day and night, that you may observe to do according to all that is written in it. For then you will make your way prosperous, and then you will have good success.

—Joshua 1:8

Abraham, the father of faith, understood and walked in the light that he had. In these End times, Yah is restoring to the church what will make us blessed, successful, and prosperous: the Torah as revealed to us by the Holy Spirit. As we meditate on Yah's holy Commandments, Judgments and Precepts, the Word will become flesh in us and will produce the fruit of obedience. Obedience will bring the fullness of the blessing.

Yeshua

Yeshua, commonly called Jesus Christ, is the real Hebrew name for the Jewish Messiah. Yeshua means Yah is our Salvation and it implies Salvation, Deliverance, and

Redemption. Throughout this book, I will only use Yeshua, His true Hebrew name.

Yeshua is the Living Torah, or the Torah made flesh. As you follow Him and His Ruach HaKodesh, His Holy Spirit, He will lead you into all truth.

And you shall know the truth, and the truth shall make you free.

—John 8:32

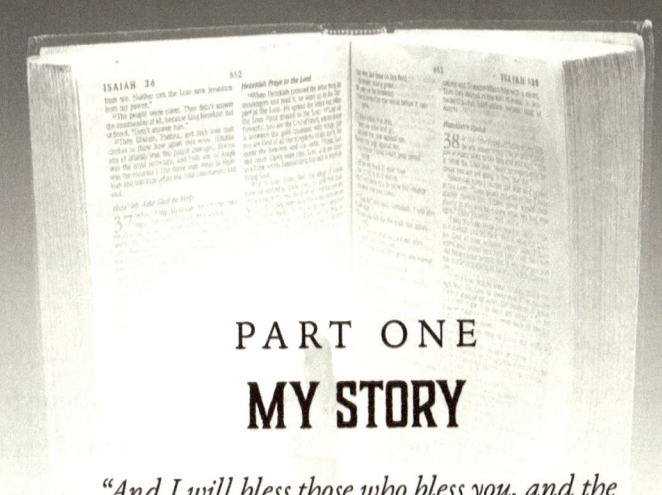

PART ONE
MY STORY

*"And I will bless those who bless you, and the
one who curses you I will curse. And in you all
the families of the earth will be blessed."*
—(Genesis 12:3)

Many years ago, I had an open vision from the LORD during my sleep. In this vision, I was a very weary soldier, walking through an endless dessert. I was dusty and you could not know what my rank was; my brown uniform had seen better days. Finally, I saw a rock and Yeshua was sitting on it. I sat next to Him very tired. He handed me a brown bag. As I opened the brown bag, there was an ancient key inside. He told me to point it to heaven, which I did. Immediately, the heavens opened up!

I understood that this was the *key* for *revival*!

It was in a brown paper bag, which seemed unfitting for such a glorious and important treasure. Most people would not even bother to look in because the wrapping seemed so unimportant. Later on, I understood that that brown paper bag represented me and our ministry, Kad-Esh MAP Ministries. It is unseemly that such a non-sophisticated ministry like ours, with such a non-impressive vessel like me, would be the housing of such an important treasure – THE KEY OF ABRAHAM that has the power to open the entire world for end time revival!

As I took the key from the LORD, He commanded me to keep moving and not to allow any weariness or fatigue to stop me. The desert seemed endless, but I obeyed. As I kept moving with quite a despondent attitude, I saw angels, very mighty angels that were flying over my head and they were whispering to each other,

"She does not know who she is."

They kept on saying this back and forth in bewilderment and wonder to each other as they were flying over my head. They did this many times! Finally, quite frustrated, I stopped and cried:

"So, who am I?

To which they answered with a deep sense of reverence and awe, *"You are the daughter of Elijah."*

To which I answered in utter distress and grief with a piercing cry, feeling totally alone and abandoned,

"If I am the daughter of Elijah, where is my father?"

After that piercing cry, I woke up with a deep pain in my heart, wondering what this dream meant.

Elijah had the authority to open and to close the heavens at his command. So, it is that because of the idolatry of Israel, he closed the heavens for three years. And after his confrontational encounter on Mount Carmel with all the 850 prophets of Baal and Ashera, the Fire of God came down on his sacrifice. After he slaughtered all the lying prophets and 'theologians' single handedly, he went to the top of Mount Carmel and opened up the heavens to the point that a great rain came upon Israel, watering the weary and parched land. Thus, the curse broke and Israel revived again. (1 Kings 18)

LET US MEET

I am a Jew of Spanish-Chilean descent, a Sephardic Jew. My ancestors were killed during the Spanish Inquisition by the Church of that time, as they refused to convert to Christianity by force. Those that managed to escape the bonfires of the Inquisition fled to Yugoslavia. During the First World War, when persecution rose again against the Jews by the Church of the time, they escaped to Chile. I made Alyah, (ascension to the Land of Israel) in 1970. My father was one of the main Zionist leaders that brought many Chilean Jews back to the land of our ancestors and a renowned scientist.

When my time came for my army service in Israel, I was chosen to be a trainer and a commander. Since then, my life was marked. I became a soldier for life! Later on, I studied for two years and became a licensed Israeli tour guide. After a terrible tragedy in my life, Yeshua began to speak to me while guiding a Catholic group of tourists through the Sea of Galilee. No one preached the gospel to me. He began speaking to me when I took my tourists to do Mass in the church of the Primacy of Saint Peter. That is the place where Yeshua entrusted Peter to Feed His sheep.

At the entrance to this place, there is a statue representing Peter with a key in his hand, according to Matthew 16:18-19:

"I also tell you, that you are Peter, and on this rock I will build my assembly, and the gates of Hades will not prevail against it. I will give to you the keys of the kingdom of heaven, and whatever you will bind on earth will be bound in heaven; and whatever you will loose on earth will be loosed in heaven."

—Matthew 16:18-19

As I joined my tourists in their Mass service, the Holy Spirit began to speak to me and said, "Dominiquae, run for your life; be baptized and be saved." I obeyed that heavenly voice and am obeying it until this day!

I could not figure out, though, what Jesus Christ has to do with us Jews? In His name, we had been persecuted, plundered and murdered for 1,600 years!

Little did I know that the LORD was calling me to apostolic ministry and that He was going to entrust me with the *key* for end time revival.

We, Jews are like Peter; we have denied Yeshua as our Messiah for a long, long time. But now, as we are repenting, He is entrusting us with the highest positions of authority in His kingdom.

The Jewish apostles – men and women are coming!

Not much later on, I met my husband, Baruch Bierman, an American Jew of Russian and German descent that had also been called to the apostolic ministry. Most of his Bierman family was exterminated during the Nazi Holocaust and their ashes, for the most part, lay in the Death Camp of Auschwitz. He carries with me THE KEY OF ABRAHAM to all the nations that we go to.

As I have walked many years with the LORD through the wearisome desert that I saw in my dream, I've always known that there is something missing in the church for *true* revival to come in and last. Finally, in 1996, God manifested what the 'Key of Abraham' meant when He 'downloaded' through me the book that is a classic today, "The Healing Power of the Roots," where I called the church worldwide to repent from anti-Semitism, to renounce the Council of Nicaea and to get re-grafted into the Olive Tree, which is Israel.

That little book of no more than 80 pages has been now translated into many languages and as many as 30,000 copies of it have been sold or given away by heavenly Distributors. It was written in Switzerland at the insistence of some saints there. When it was first printed in English and then in German, it caused some major leaders of the Swiss renewal and other leaders, such a violent reaction that they wanted to immediately set up a Jerusalem Council #2 like in Acts 15! Even some Israeli Pastors were bewildered by it as the book called for repentance and also to consider that the laws of the Creator are still for today and they are not obsolete or done away with as Matthew 5:17-19 also states.

I was awed; the church had been divorced for so long from her original foundations with the Jewish people and so many theological books had been written; in fact, entire treatises had been written advocating the doctrines of demons and men. There are so many *large* volumes that have been published, in order to support Christianity and replacement theology, which has caused the murder of millions of Jews since the 4th century! And no one had really risen up to seriously oppose to the point that it would shake the body of Messiah worldwide! And here, a thin, insignificant looking book of less than 80 pages inspired by heaven itself could cause such a reaction?

Later on, the Father would speak to me and say: *"Dominiquae, I did not call theologians to rule my body, I called Apostles."* And Apostles stir up things, confront lies and build foundations – solid foundations.

Since 1988, there has been a prophetic movement going on. This prophetic movement has come in the Spirit of Elijah to prepare the way for the second coming of Messiah. They have been prophesying for many years now, that the Apostles are coming! That they are ushering the apostolic, but what they have all missed is that the true apostolic move began in Jerusalem with Jewish apostles and that so it shall be in these End of times; Jewish apostles together with grafted in Gentiles; men and women will carry the *key* for the revival and the restoration of all nations. As Romans 11: 15 says,

"The acceptance of the Jews (into the church) is life from the dead (Revival)"

This prophetic movement should have been fathering the emerging Jewish apostles like me, but instead, they for the most part have been too enamored with the gifts of the Spirit to really be concerned about restoring the Jewish people.

Most of these prophetic ministries have been prophesying many true things, but without clarity or substance; because they have overlooked the importance of restoring the church to its original Jewish foundations. They have been prophesying that we need to be like the early church and have a release of holiness, signs, wonders and miracles. But they have forgotten that the early church was Jewish! They have been prophesying a paradigm shift but have not known that it is about returning back to the Jewish roots of the church and repenting from all replacement theology! They have talked about a civil war in the church but did not know what the issue would be. They should have been fathering the Jewish apostles, but they could not because they were still steeped in replacement theology themselves!

That is why I cried in my dream, *"Where is my father, Elijah?"* Where are those true Prophets of God that confront the lies of replacement theology? And father the Jewish apostles?

I am one of these end time Jewish apostles and I carry THE KEY OF ABRAHAM. I look like a 'brown paper bag' but I carry within me a great treasure. It is a heavy key and it has cost me all in my life to carry it, but now, the time has come to point it to heaven for a great end time revival, followed with the most astounding signs, wonders and miracles and the salvation of many sheep nations and ethnic groups and tribes. Many indigenous people that have suffered at the hands of Christianity will take this key and will outrun Western Christians as they get back from this Jewish woman, the fullness of the lost and forgotten gospel of the kingdom. Whoever will receive this key and pay the price to carry it and use it, will be a *point of contact* for revival in churches, cities, regions and nations.

Will you be a point of contact and receive this awesome *key*, though it is handed to you in a 'paper bag'?

"Many peoples shall go and say, Come you, and let us go up to the mountain of Yahveh, to the house of the God of Jacob; and he will teach us of his ways, and we will walk in his paths: for out of Zion shall go forth the law, and the Word of Yahveh from Jerusalem."

—Isaiah 2:3

"Thus says Yahveh of Hosts: In those days [it shall happen], that ten men shall take hold, out of all the languages of the nations, they shall take hold of the skirt (hem, fringes) of him who is a Jew, saying, We will go with you, for we have heard that God is with you."

—Zachariah 8:23

Important

As you read this book and you find terminology that you do not understand, please go immediately to the appendixes at the end and you will find the explanations. Also, I encourage you to read my previous books (See list at the end of this book).

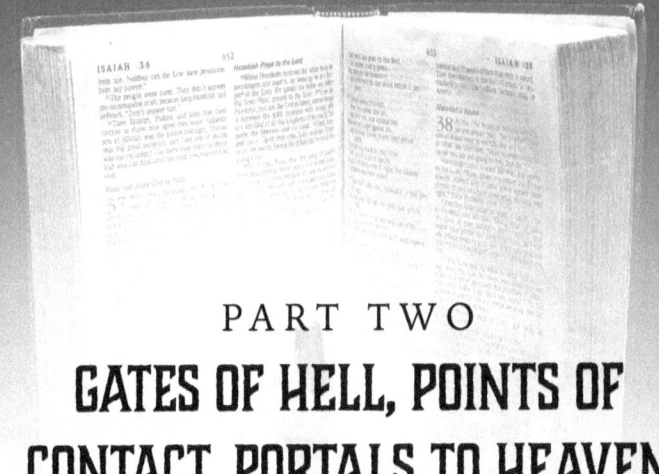

PART TWO
GATES OF HELL, POINTS OF CONTACT, PORTALS TO HEAVEN

"He said to them, "But who do you say that I am?" Simon Peter answered, "You are the Messiah, the Son of the living God." Yeshua answered him, "Blessed are you, Simon Bar-Jonah, for flesh and blood has not revealed this to you, but my Father who is in heaven. I also tell you, that you are Peter, and on this rock I will build my assembly, and the gates of Hades will not prevail against it."
—Matthew 16:15-18

GATES OF HELL

1. Gates of hell are actual places where there is active interaction between the demonic realm and earth. Places in the earth from which demonic activity is released. Most pagan shrines are gates of hell. There are mystical places that people pilgrim into such as Mecca, (the Kava or Black Stone that Moslems worship), Katmandu in India, which is

a center of New Age, Safed in Israel, which is a center for Kabala and 'Jewish Mysticism', Salt Lake City, which is a center for cultic Mormon studies and secret researches. All Masonic lodges and secret societies lodges.

2. Gates of hell are places where there have been great slaughters and spilling of innocent blood. Such as abortion clinics, death camps such as Auschwitz, Sobibor, Treblinka and Majdanek in Poland. All places where people were killed in the name of Christianity such as native land all over the world, places where blood was spilt during the Crusades, the Spanish Inquisition, etc. From those places, the blood of the victims cries out from the ground, bringing a curse on that place and marking it with the 'Mark of Cain'. There is no presence of the Lord and no rest there. This is the reason why Spain, Germany and all of Europe have not been able to enjoy revival for so long. There is too much Jewish blood crying out from the ground.

3. Gates of hell are any places where there has been in the past or there are in the present, altars to foreign gods, satanic worship places, witches covens, New Age and Mystical, witchcraft shops and businesses, Places of Spiritual Reading, like palm readers, coffee and tobacco leaves readers, iridology, shamans, witch doctors and healers. Any place where there is a person that is a 'contact point' for spiritual demonic activity such as mediums and channelers, diviners, crystal balls, etc... Also, places of alternative medicine such as reflexology, acupuncture, yoga and meditation. Every place of immorality such as porn shops and prostitution houses.

Every place where spirits are invoked or channeled such as metal rock concerts, rock CD's, music and video shops where all these things are displayed and sold. Gates of hell can be inside family houses, in forests, shops, clubs, bars, restaurants or community and worship centers.

In Matthew 16:15-19, Yeshua said that the revelation of who He is was going to be the rock on which we would stand in order to exercise spiritual authority over the gates of hell. As we stand on the revelation of His identity as Jewish Messiah, we can exercise all of His authority and render the gates of hell inactive and actually close them!

The reason why the Ecclesia has had very little authority to close these gates is because she has not known Yeshua as a Jew. She has not known His true name and has not used it and she has had a wrong idea of who He is. Because the revelation of His identity has been so dim, so the power and authority has been very limited. That is the reason why there is not one nation/tribe/ethnic group fully saved after almost 2,000 years of supposed gospel.

When the church expelled the Jews and divorced from the Jewish roots and from the Jewish Messiah in 325, through the Council of Nicaea, and established Christianity as a state religion, it *opened up a major gate of hell within her.* Through replacement theology, evil spirits were activated *from within her* to bring stealing, killing and destruction (the opposite of what Yeshua came to bring according to John 10:10!) to the Jewish people and later, to all indigenous peoples that were conquered by the Western Christian countries, like Africa,

North and South America, Alaska, Australia, New Zealand, the Caribbean, etc.Since replacement theology (the church replaces Israel, pagan feasts the holy feasts and religious traditions the Commandments of God) has harbored the principality of *anti-Mesitojuz** called by many wrongly, anti-Semitism, then the point of contact for this hideous principality is the church herself as long as she stills harbors replacement theology.**

She is the channeler of the spirits that functioned during the Nazi Holocaust. Notice that Germany was the most Protestant nation in the world in 1933 and Poland was the most Catholic! So, the Christians both Protestant and Catholics were the *point of contact* to open a wider gate of hell in Europe and to channel those murderous spirits of destruction. Hitler received the blessings of the Pope, the Bishops and the highest clergy officials of both Catholic and Protestant/Lutheran church, when he rose to power in 1933. That also explains the very distressful fact that *not one* Christian organization or denomination rose up with one voice to oppose Hitler. The church had already been a demonic *point of contact* for evil spirits of destruction to be channeled through her against the Jewish people!

---

* *The anti-Mesitojuz* is a demonic principlaity with five heads: anti-Mesiah, anti-Israel, anti-Torah, anti-Jewish, and anti-Zionist.

** *Replacement theology* is the theology that belives the church replaces Israel as God's chosen people, however we find in Romans 11 that the church grafts into Israel. Read my book *Grafted In* for more: www.kad-esh. org/shop

Gates of Hell are opened by Unholy Contract, Vows or Covenants

The contract that opened the Gates of Hell through the Church was the Council of Nicaea. This demonic document was authored by Constantine in the year 325 AD, and signed by most of the Gentile Church fathers of the 4th century. This document called all the Gentile believers to 'separate themselves from the detestable company of the Jews' and to establish a replacement system of festivals that followed 'the convenient course of the days of the week' rather than the Hebrew calendar. This call of separation of the Jews and everything Jewish, banished the Jewish Messiah outside of this Church and with Him, of course, the Holy Spirit also. Thus, the Dark Ages set in upon this Church because she became a seat and a channeler of spirits of darkness that have stolen, killed and destroyed many Jewish people and some other indigenous people in the name of Christ. This contract with hell, called the Council of Nicaea, ushered the Church into a place of great strife and division, since those spirits were given free rule after expelling the Jewish people and separating from the *God-given points of contact for the salvation of the nations* – namely, the People of the Covenant (both covenants!), the Jewish people!

During the 16th century, God raised up a point of contact called Martin Luther that attempted to close the gates of hell which were opened in 325 AD; however, he only had partial revelation. He was lifted up in pride and thought that he knew better than anyone else and thus attempted to evangelize the

Jews. Since the Jews had been murdered and plundered for too long in the name of Christianity, they rejected Luther's attempts. Martin Luther got offended by their rejection of him and his more 'enlightened' Christianity and wrote a book that became a bigger *point of contact for the church to be the seat of the spirits of darkness that kill Jews*. In His book "On the Jews and their lies," Luther gave his 'honest opinion' on how to get rid from the 'devilish plague called the Jews' beginning with burning their books of Talmud, continuing with burning their synagogues, killing their rabbis, devoiding them from traveling privileges, confiscating their possessions, forbidding them to study. He wrote that his purpose is to completely 'get rid of this demonic plague called the Jews". Later on, Adolph Hitler during his terror Nazi rule from Germany, wrote a book called "*Mein Kampf*" or "*My Battle*," where he penned the Final Solution that managed to exterminate most of Europe's Jewry, over six million people and among them over 11/2 million children in the gas chambers, ovens and the crematoriums of Poland. Hitler wrote in his book that he was only following the instructions of Martin Luther, and indeed, all the steps that he took leading to the final extermination were in perfect order according to Martin Luther's instructions. Many of the Nazi executors were baptized Lutherans or Protestants.

So, we have *two major points of contact* that have caused the church to open Gates of Hell: Constantine with his Council of Nicaea in the 4th century and Martin Luther with his book "On the Jews and their lies" in the 16th century, who became a point of contact for Hitler and his final solution of extermination of all Jews. Those were the vows and the contracts made with the devil to bring destruction through the church to the Jews. There are many more that have fueled these with their writings such as John Chrysostom, Saint Augustine and too many others to mention up to the 21st century!

POINTS OF CONTACT

"It happened, when the king had heard the words of the book of the law, that he tore his clothes."

—2 Kings 22:10

I have already mentioned that a point of contact is a *person* who, through a vow or a covenant, opens a way for spirits to come through. This point of contact can be a Godly person or an ungodly person. Also, these points of contact can be the vessel for demonic spirits or for the Holy Spirit, depending on the vows and the covenants that are made. In the case of Luther, he began as a Godly point of contact and then through pride and offence, he was given over to vows with the devil and the results are devastating until today.

In 2 Kings 22, we see that young King Josiah became a point of contact for the last revival in Judah before the exile to Babylon. He rent his clothes when they found the Book of the Torah (Law) under the debris of the Temple and made a Covenant with Yah (God) to destroy all the gates of hell or high places of pagan worship.

Points of contact that open gates or portals are always covenant people; they are committed either to God or to the devil, but they are fully committed! All true revivalists have been fully committed covenant people; thus, they became contact points to open portals to heaven. Those open heavens above their areas and wherever they went caused revival to break forth. When you connect or covenant with a point of contact, you become a point of contact.

For example, Cornelius, a Gentile, covenanted with the main points of contact, which were assigned by Yah (God), the Jewish people; the most ancient covenant people. As he gave to them and prayed for them continually, a *memorial* came before God who in turn visited Cornelius (A portal to heaven was opened in Caesarea) and sent him another Jew as a contact point – Simon Peter. Cornelius became a heavenly gate opener for the Gentiles when he blessed the Jews! (Acts 10)

This explains the following Scripture:

"Again I say unto you, that if two of you shall agree on earth as touching anything that they shall ask, it shall be done for them of my Father who is in heaven."

—Mathew 18:19

This is what happens when two covenant people become points of contact in agreement. The heavens open up and prayer is answered.

Who chooses the points of contact? God does and His first points of contact to open blessing and revival are the Jews. 'To the Jew first' applies to everything, (Romans 1:16, Romans 2:9, 10) but also grafted in Gentiles are called to be points of contact. In fact, we are all called to walk so committed and covenanted with Yah *that we may all be points of contact* for opening portals of heaven (1 Peter 2:9). Every one of our homes should be portals of heaven. And every one of our congregational halls, schools and businesses. But for that, we need to cleanse from every lie and destructive theology that we have believed and sanctify our spaces from all immorality and idolatry and any Mixture! I believe that the true Bride of the Messiah is called to be a point of contact for the lost and a portal to heaven, where free interaction between heaven and earth and demonstrations of the Spirit happen all the time. But replacement theology has been blocking the Ecclesia from fully becoming this portal and gateway to heaven that she is called to be.

There are two major types of points of contact:

• *Points of contact for revival* are people of covenant and commitment; their mere presence opens the Portals of heaven.

• *Points of contact for making restitution* so that curses will break, and *favor* can be restored, can be any wronged party. For example, Holocaust survivors among the Jews are always right points of contact for restitution by Christian Germans and by Christians in general, since Hitler was riding upon the common Jew hatred in Christianity and replacement theology in order to set the stage for the Holocaust. All Jews in general are always right points of contact for Christians to repent to, ask forgiveness and make restitution and bless for curses to be broken throughout the Church and the nations. In the case of places where first nations, indigenous people were wronged, all indigenous people are points of contact for repentance and restitution at any and all times. However, the chiefs of the tribes are excellent points of contact in order to forgive, break curses and release a more powerful blessing.

THE MOST POWERFUL END TIME CONTACT POINTS

"Thus says Yahveh of Hosts: In those days [it shall happen], that ten men shall take hold, out of all the languages of the nations, they shall take hold of the skirt (tsitsit or fringes-represent God's Commandments) of him who is a Jew, saying, We will go with you, for we have heard that God is with you."
—Zechariah 8:23

These are redeemed and apostolic Jews – Jewish apostles that walk in the power of the covenant and carry with them an anointing to destroy the gates of hell, which were established by Constantine through the Council of Nicaea.

Their mere presence causes all the gates of hell to tremble and they stir up change and repentance wherever they go. They are both a contact point for portals of heaven and revival to open up and also excellent contact points for restitution, as they are all survivors of Christian persecution. The Sephardic or Spanish Jews are survivors of the Spanish Inquisition and the Ashkenazi Jews are survivors of the

Eastern European pogroms and the Nazi Holocaust; nevertheless, both groups of Jews and their ancestors have suffered in the hands of Christianity on all sides.

Because the church has affected all the nations with replacement theology (the church replaces Israel, pagan feasts the holy feasts and religious traditions the Commandments of God) and through it, ANTI-MESITOJUZ (a 5 headed principality wrongly called Anti-Semitism) and Jew hatred, all nations would profit from the visit and the connection with Zachariah 8:23 type of Jews.

As the church in any area receives them, repents to them, makes restitution in practical ways, they have the power of breaking national curses and curses over entire regions; thus, changing the atmosphere completely and preparing the stage for revival.

They also carry the authority of instructing the church in the true gospel of the kingdom that has been forgotten for over 1800 since Origen brought Greek philosophy into the church after the Jewish apostles died. Their authority in the Scriptures is obvious and their words generate change and transformation. They have the anointing of restorers and are accompanied by signs, wonders and many miracles of restoration.

Israeli Apostolic Jews

They are the most powerful of all Zachariah 8:23 points of contact as they are themselves already fully restored to the promise of the covenant with Israel, which includes the

Land of Israel. And among the Israeli Jews, those that are sent out of Jerusalem, that is the seat of government for Israel and called to be the throne of the LORD in Jeremiah 3:17 and also as Isaiah 2:1-3 says *"For out of Zion will come out the Law and the Word of the LORD from Jerusalem."* Just like the apostolic government of the early church was in Jerusalem, so it will be with the end time glorious church!

The move is still young but as the church in all nations begins to pray earnestly for these Israeli Jews, they will rise up more and more and fulfill their calling to become points of contact for revival and to be a light unto the nations through their wholesome teachings of Torah and Spirit.

The point of separation of the church was at the level of the Messianic Jews of the 4th century. So, the point of contact for its unification, are the Messianic Jews of the 21st century that restore the Torah, the understanding of the Hebrew scriptures to the nations. How will you recognize them? They carry a weight of authority, stir up change, you cannot ignore that they are in town. They teach the scriptures with unprecedented clarity, they provoke a response and are followed with signs, wonders and miracles. (They are not your normal guest minister or motivational speaker.)

PORTALS TO HEAVEN

"And he dreamed. And behold, a ladder set up on the earth, and the top of it reached to heaven. And behold, the angels of God ascending and descending on it."

—Genesis 28:12

Those are places where there is free interaction between heaven and earth; where it is very easy to pray and receive divine revelation. Since the authority to defeat the gates of hell comes from a place of revelation of the Messiah's identity, those portals to heaven are where revelation comes in and equips the saints with that authority. The holy angels of God always 'camp' at the portals to heaven. You will know that you are in a portal when you experience more revelation and prophetic dreams in that place. Whenever people have slept in my home or especially in my prayer room, they always report that they had a prophetic dream, a revelation or a visitation and also in our congregational hall and MAP Center (Messianic-Apostolic-Prophetic) in Israel. Most guests have reported prophetic dreams, divine revelations or an experience with the Holy Spirit. Sometimes, it is manifested in deep inner healings, deliverances or physical healings.

A portal to heaven can be anywhere in our homes, private prayer place, a congregational hall where people are committed to praying and fasting for revival. The key for opening portals of heaven is that there are committed and covenanted contact points there that keep the portal open through prayer, worship and sacrifice. Abraham set up such places when he sacrificed to Elohim in Bethel and in Beer Sheba (Genesis 12:8, Genesis 13:4, Genesis 28:20, Genesis 31:13, Genesis 35:1,10,11, Genesis 21:15-19, 31-33, Genesis 26:23-25, Genesis 28:10-16). Everytime he passed by, he revisited the place and so did his descendants.

Pastor Seymour, a black pastor, set up such a place in Azusa Street in Los Angeles, almost 100 years ago and that is when the Pentecostal movement was released! Pastor David Yonggi Cho set his up over South Korea as he opened the place of his congregational hall for 24 hour prayer and his people became a living sacrifice. After three years of this heavenly interaction, healing miracles began to happen by themselves in his congregation, without anyone laying on hands or praying. The *Shechina,* or manifested glory of Yah accompanied with His holy angels had found a place of rest.

Jerusalem, the capital of Israel, the city of the King is the strongest portal of heaven that there is on earth; she is called the throne of the LORD! (Jeremiah 3:17). And especially Mount Moriah that is the Temple Mount. This is the reason why every ruling empire has set their hearts to conquer Jerusalem and to build altars of foreign worship on the Temple Mount. Any ruling empire that has Jerusalem and sets his seat of worship on the Temple Mount has authority to influence the nations. When the Greeks established worship to Jupiter up there and sacrificed pigs on the altar, they influenced all nations with Greek culture and ruled the nations. When a small amount of Jews from the Maccabean family dared to defy the Greek Empire and took the Temple back from the Greek, against all odds, and sanctified it, it weakened the Greek Empire until it was defeated by the Romans. (Hanukkah is the feast of dedication that Yeshua celebrated and that commemorates this event, John 10:22).

This is the sole purpose of the Palestinian uprising (Intifada); it is to possess the portals of heaven. (Which are many in Israel such as Hebron, Bethel, Beersheba, etc.) And most particularly, the Temple Mount. The uprising began when Prime Minister Ariel Sharon dared to go up to the Temple Mount as a Jew to pray prior to the elections. The favor of God fell upon him right after this and he was elected and won by a 'landslide'. At the same time, the Palestinian uprising began as a reaction. It is important to note that though the Moslems have built their shrines on the Temple Mount, this is the former place of the Holy Temple of Yahveh, built by Solomon, the place were Abraham offered Isaac on the altar and the covenant of exchange happened (Genesis 22), the seat of the government of Israel when in covenant with Yah (God) and the future seat of the third temple and the throne of the LORD on earth. Thus, it is not surprising that every time that Yeshua came to Jerusalem, He taught at the Temple. Since the miraculous six day war of June 1967, the Temple Mount is officially and legally, Israeli territory, though religious autonomy has been given to the Wakf or the Moslem authorities.

As in Isaiah 14:12-15, Satan is always trying to sit on the throne of the Most High and usurp His place, lifting himself up above the Creator. Thus, he always tries to take over the portals of heaven where Yahveh (the I AM) is worshipped! That is the reason why revivals die, because the places of revival are taken over by spirits of darkness that come in through many cracks such as:

- Strife among the saints and the covenanted people.
- Jealousy and power contests.
- Pride and offences.
- Replacement theology and rejection of the Jewish roots.
- Resisting points of contact.
- Rebellion against God's rule, building man's empires.
- Discrimination against women in leadership positions.
- Stifling Davidic worship.
- Any kind of racism.
- Active sin and immorality.

A portal to heaven can be and needs to be redeemed through repentance, sanctification, prayer, worship and sacrifice.

ICHABOD

Ichabod, is when the glory departs from a portal of heaven, like in Shiloh when the Ark of the Covenant was taken by the Philistines and the glory departed from Israel because of the apostasy of Eli and his wicked sons (1 Samuel 4:21).

Ichabod happened in the church because of the establishing of the Council of Nicaea and Christianity as a state religion.

The Messianic Jews were expelled; Shabbat and the holy feasts and commandments were rejected. The glory departed from the church; signs, wonders and miracles ceased and darkness, superstition and murder set in.

Until this day, Yah (the LORD) is restoring His *Kabod*, His glory to His Bride as she comes out of the theologies of Christianity into the original gospel of the kingdom, with its Hebrew foundations. This process of sanctification has been going on in high gear since 1906 when the Pentecostal revival began and the baptism of the Holy Spirit was restored. As she has advanced in the process of sanctification and restoration to truth, holiness and power, she is now ready for the end time move of restoration to the original apostolic Jewish foundations as the early church had when the Jewish apostles were alive. As she is restored back to the original foundation with Israel as grafted into the Olive Tree (Romans 11:11-19), she will be able to go forward and possess the nations. Those that will reject this end time move of repentance and restoration to the Hebrew foundations and will refuse to be grafted in will die in the desert of their rebellion and erroneous Christian theologies (Psalm 68:6). Time is very late; the nations are not saved. Israel is in great struggles for survival. Nature is groaning with earthquakes and floods for the Sons of God to be revealed. The blood of the Jews and all slaughtered by Christianity is crying out from the earth, entire regions have been closed from revival because of this.

One time, I was walking with one of my prayer groups through the death camps of Poland. We were in the forest of Sobibor, where many Jews were exterminated. There were many unmarked graves on the ground and the land had remains of many ashes and powdered human bones. We were all walking in silence. There was no one else there, and then I heard it. I clearly heard cries, piercing cries, distressed and terrified cries of men, women and children. I stopped, deeply shaken by those piercing cries and I asked the rest of the team, "Did you hear something?" They had all heard the same horrifying cries! Then we realized that the blood of our Jewish brethren was crying out from the ground like the blood of Abel! God's ears are not deaf to the cry of the blood, and he is ready to judge the nations because of it (Isaiah 34). But judgment must first begin in the house of God (1 Peter 4:17). It is through the church that these Jew hating doctrines have been established in the nations. The church worldwide, all denominations are called to accountability because of these deathly doctrines and are called to repentance for their sins and the sins of past generations.

"And He said, what have you done? The voice of your brother's blood cries to Me from the ground."

—Genesis 4:10.

The LORD is separating the Sheep from the Goats! (Matthew 25:32-33) And the Tares from the Wheat. (Matthew 13:36-43)

CONCLUSION

Zechariah 8:23 talks about the redeemed Jewish apostles, being the contact points for open heavens for this end time revival of restoration.

"Thus says Yahveh of Hosts: In those days [it shall happen], that ten men shall take hold, out of all the languages of the

nations, they shall take hold of the skirt (hem and fringes, the Tsitsit of Numbers 15:38) of him who is a Jew, saying, We will go with you, for we have heard that God is with you."

—Zechariah 8:23

Paraphrase: "Let us go with you (covenant with you) because we have heard that God is with you (portals to heaven are opened wherever you go)"

For 1,600 years, the church has killed and rejected the very ones that have brought her and have the power to bring her and the nations the blessing. She has killed the major contact points for revival. The word in Romans 11:15, promises that the acceptance of these contact points (Redeemed Jews) is life from the dead or revival. Zechariah 8:23 confirms it as Gentiles connect and covenant with these apostolic Jews by firmly taking hold of the fringes of their garment, which represent their covenant of obedience to God's commandments and the place from which instruction in righteousness and healing flows.

"Speak to the children of Israel, and bid those who they make them fringes in the borders of their garments throughout their generations, and that they put on the fringe of each border a cord of blue: and it shall be to you for a fringe, that you may look on it, and remember all the commandments of Yahveh, and do them; and that you not follow after your own heart and your own eyes, after which you use to play the prostitute;

that you may remember and do all my commandments, and be holy to your God."

—Numbers 15:38-40

This end time revival is summarized best in Malachi 4 where it says that the Sun of righteousness will arise with healing in his 'wings,' which in Hebrew is *"Knafeicha"* or the *fringes* (*tsitsit*, see Numbers 15:38) of His garment. How will the Sun of righteousness arise? Through His end time chosen points of contact apostolic/Messianic Jews that are being sent to the nations to teach the truth, reverse the curses and bring the healing that the nations need. It is therefore no surprise that in Malachi, the instruction is *remember* the law of Moses (the very books that have been forbidden by Christianity and called "Old Testament" since the Council of Nicaea). And then "Elijah will come and turn the hearts of the fathers to the children and the children to the fathers". If this does not happen, a terrible curse will smite the earth. We have already seen the warnings of that curse as the Twin Towers fell in New York, the many hurricanes that hit Florida in 2004 and the terrible Tsunami wave and earthquake that has killed over 200,000 people on Christmas weekend in 2004.

Whatever church, tribe, nation group, denomination or individual that will connect with the chosen end time Jewish contact points, covenant and partner with them, will see portals to heaven opened and gates to hell closed. They bring a full revelation of who the Messiah is and with it all the authority necessary (that has been lost since the Council of Nicaea) to defeat the gates of hell and save the nations.

"I will bless them that bless you, curse them that curse you and in you all the families of the earth will be blessed."

—Genesis 12:3

How can you open a portal to heaven and close the gates of hell in your area?

These instructions will work anywhere there are churches or Christianity. In order to prepare an area for revival, *it must begin* with the church first. As judgment begins in the house of God, also revival begins in the house of God and moves on to the unsaved peoples. Therefore, for this end time revival, the church must get rid of all replacement theology, renounce the Council of Nicaea and reconnect back with the Jews and the Jewish roots of the faith. This is the *end time master key* for revival and the salvation of many sheep nations. It is called THE *KEY OF ABRAHAM* and it is based on Genesis 12:3, which is the key scripture for the blessing and salvation of all the families and ethnic groups of the earth, *if* they bless and honor the Jewish people. And most particularly, the redeemed Jews that are now taking their rightful position of authority within the church worldwide as the original fathers and mothers of the faith. Jealousy and pride against them culminated in the Council of Nicaea, so humility and acceptance will bring them back and set the stage for end time revival (Romans 11:15). They will team up with grafted in Gentiles and *together,* they will reach out to all the nations with the end time gospel of the kingdom.

PRACTICAL APPLICATIONS

1. *Set apart* a place of worship and prayer.
2. *Commit to pray and seek YAH* until He rains righteousness on you and your area. Until revival comes.
3. *Begin to repent* from all traces of replacement theology. *Break your vow* with the Council of Nicaea,* with Constantine and Martin Luther's erroneous teachings against the Jews and against the law of God. (See Appendix #3)
4. *Ask for God's forgiveness* for rejecting the Jews and the Jewish roots of the faith. You may ask for forgiveness for the sins of past generations. Remember that all the curses in the nations come from dishonoring and harming the Jewish people. (Isaiah 34, Genesis 12:3, Zechariah 2:6)
5. *Connect/covenant and partner* with end time apostolic Jews as contact points. Bring them to your area, so they can break the curses and release the blessing.
6. *Make restitution* to the Jews through these contact points by loving, praying and supporting them financially, so the blessing can come to your area. Remember: they are contact points that have the

---

* *The Council of Nicea* was the council of Roman bishops that created the legal, religious, and political division from the Jewish roots of the faith in 325 AD. Please see the appendix for more information.

power to break the curses and release the blessings, but lip service is not enough! The Jews have been plundered by Christianity and the nations for too long; so, practical steps of giving and restoration of honor need to be established. (Remember, 2 Samuel 21 how King David had to make restitution to the Gibeonites because of the sins of King Saul).

7. *Commit to be instructed* by them. They are God-given contact points to open the full revelation of the Word and of Messiah that has been missing since the Council of Nicaea. Remember that revelation is the key for authority to defeat the gates of hell!

8. *Take authority.* Broad base of authority is established as the original Jewish foundation of the faith is restored through revelation; you can go ahead and use that authority to close (bind and forbid) the gates of hell that are open in your area, where there is demonic activity.

9. *Remember* that you will have to repent on behalf of the sins of your ancestors and past generations for sins committed in the land where you are. (Ezekiel 22:30)

10. *Take all the steps of repentance.* If the sins were committed against the first nations and indigenous people of that land, you will have to take all the steps of repentance, renouncing and restitution to them so that they might release the blessing on the Land.

11. *Keep the portals of heaven open* through acts of prayer, worship and sacrificial giving into your points of contact and wherever else Yah will lead.
12. *Keep your heart humble, obedient and teachable.* All revivals die because of pride and jealousy. Remember that God gives grace to the humble, but He resists the proud! (James 4:6,7)

"For the acceptance of the Jews is life from the dead"

—Romans 11:15

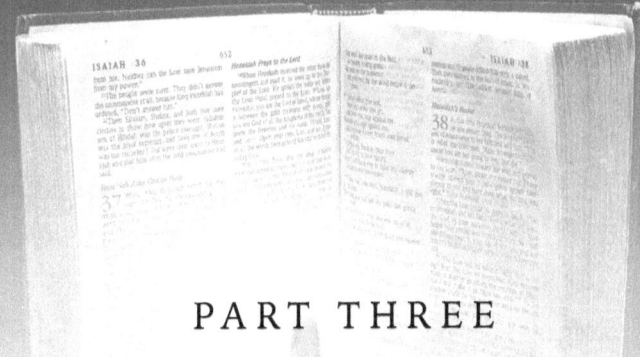

PART THREE
OPENING PORTALS OF HEAVEN

"Solomon offered for the sacrifice of peace-offerings, which he offered to Yahveh, two and twenty thousand oxen, and one hundred twenty thousand sheep. So the king and all the children of Israel dedicated the house of Yahveh."

—1 Kings 8:63

The best example of how to open a portal to heaven is found in 1 Kings Chapters 1 to 8; when King Solomon makes the decision to build a house for Yahveh (the LORD) on Mount Moriah.

Why Mount Moriah? That was the place where the covenant of exchange happened between Abraham and Elohim in Genesis 22. Abraham was willing to *sacrifice his only son,*Isaac,the one that he waited for, for so long. He was the one who carried all the promise. Without whom the life of Abraham would end in futility. Abraham went to *worship Yah and to sacrifice to Yah on Mount Moriah.* the LORD intervened at the last moment and prevented him from sacrificing Isaac and He provided a ram instead. There was no need for Abraham to give his son in order to ratify the covenant with the Creator. He would provide, and not only a ram, but later on at the fullness of time; He would provide His Son to open the heavens for all mankind with one extravagant sacrifice in Calvary, in Jerusalem! And this *is the covenant of exchange* that happened on Mount Moriah that later on became the site of the Holy Temple and today it is still called the Temple Mount. (Genesis 22)

Through Abraham's willingness to do this extravagant sacrifice of his only son, he opened the gate of heaven for God's Son to be given in the fullness of time.

The visitation of the angel that stopped Abraham was a sign of an open heavens. Abraham managed to attract the attention of the Almighty by his willingness to sacrifice all. And he opened a portal to heaven that would never close.

Later on, King Solomon would build the Holy Temple there; a place of rest for the Shechina, the manifested presence and glory of God. He would place the Ark of the Covenant in the holy of holiest, a sign of favor to all of Israel. Yahveh would be sitting Himself as a King on Mount Moriah between the wings of the Cherubim. This eventually caused Israel to become the first superpower of her time!

Kings and Queens from far lands would come and pay homage to the King of Kings and to the human king that would be sitting on the throne of David. While this principal portal of heaven was open, Israel enjoyed favor and prosperity. The people were happy about their lives!

Though Abraham opened this portal, it was King Solomon that re-opened it. He first prepared a glorious house for the Almighty.

He dedicated it in prayer and then he sacrificed 20,000 heifers and 120,000 sheep to Yah! This was a huge sacrifice. That did it! The Almighty answered with His voice and His kabod (His glory). He entered the house and rested there.

The glory of God was upon Israel and Solomon's reign because of this extravagant act of worship and sacrifice! (1 Kings 9)

POINTS OF CONTACT

We can see here that in Genesis 22, the point of contact to open a portal to heaven was Abraham and the *means* was his willingness to do the *extravagant sacrifice* of his only son, Isaac. And in 1 Kings 8, the point of contact was King Solomon and his *extravagant sacrifice* of 20,000 heifers and 120,000 sheep. We will recognize this pattern all over the Scriptures.

Great giving opens the portals of heaven over regions and nations.

Can you imagine such a great BBQ? The Cohanim (Priest) and the Levites had more than enough for their needs, and they could share their food with all of Israel. After all, who can eat so much meat? After this extravagant sacrifice, the portal was maintained open by the continual morning and evening worship, sacrifice and the Shabbat and holy convocations seven-fold sacrifices.

Sacrifices out of a heart of worship keep the portals of heaven open!

STOPPING THE PLAGUE

In a previous occasion in 2 Samuel 26, we see that God had plagued Israel because King David did a count on the people, which was not appointed. For three days, the plague had killed 70,000 people in Israel. King David was distressed as the people were suffering because of his sin. The destroying angel finally stopped over the threshing floor of a man by the name of Araunah, the Jebusite. As David was *praying* and begging God for mercy for the people and for the plague to stop, Gad the prophet came and gave David *the key:*

"Rise up and sacrifice to Yah (the LORD)".

King David rose up and went to the threshing floor over which the destroying angel was waiting. The owner gladly agreed to give King David the place for a sacrifice, but the king did not receive the gift but rather bought it! What was the king's reason?

"No, but I will surely buy it from you for a price, for *I will not offer burnt offerings to the LORD that cost me nothing.* So David bought the threshing floor and the oxen for fifty shekels of silver. David built an altar there to the LORD and offered there burnt offerings and peace offerings thus *the LORD was moved by prayer for the land and the plague was held back from Israel."*

—2 Samuel 26:24,25

Do you know why God is not moved by our prayers for revival? Because there is no sacrificial giving with it. We pray and worship and sing, but nothing much happens; the plague is still in the land, portals of heaven do not open up. Sacrificial and extravagant giving from a heart of honor and worship are needed.

Who was the contact point for the portal to be opened over the threshing floor of Araunah? King David himself who caused this plague by his sin, he also *paid* to stop it! And Yah listened!

TO THE JEW FIRST

Do you know that there is a plague in the Church? A plague that has been killing Jews and has caused millions of Christians to be broken off the Olive Tree according to Romans 11:19? This plague has been killing the nations for lack of salvation.

There is not even one sheep nation in sight? Why? Because of the sins of the church towards the people of the covenant; the Jewish people. It has caused entire nations to shut to revival, and the church is still going in circles trying to find the door, trying to find the Key.

And the key is THE KEY OF ABRAHAM!

"I will bless them that bless thee and curse them that curse thee"
—Genesis 12:3

In order to stop the plague of sin, unbelief and death in the church and in the nations, it is time to rise up and *pray* first for Israel and Jerusalem, (Psalm 122:6) above all other prayers, and accompany those prayers with *extravagant, sacrificial giving* to the Jews, those Contact points for revival!

The entire church should be making extravagant restitution to the Jewish people, beginning with the Messianic Jews!

Every church should adopt a Messianic ministry, a Messianic congregations and should pour blessings and sacrificial giving with no strings attached.

Jewish apostles should be honored by laying sacrificial gifts, lands,houses, cars and offerings at their feet with no strings attached!

For many years, some well-meaning Christians have been trying to bless the Messianic Jews, by letting them use buildings that they purchase for ministry in Israel. But they always retain the title and the ownership; they are always retaining the control. That is very wrong giving; it is actually dishonoring. I have had situations when Christians in the nations have tried to give me money for the purchase of the building for the ministry or for other things. However, any time that they desired to give the money with the condition of retaining any part in ownership or registration of the building, I have refused the offering. The Jewish people have been plundered for so long; it is time to give to them without reservation! It is time to honor them like the Jewish apostles were honored in Jerusalem as people laid the gifts at their feet. After all, the Jewish people are the original church fathers and mothers and they should be honored as such!

After all, the Dark Ages set in, in the church when the Messianic Jews were dishonored and expelled out of it after the Council of Nicaea was signed by the church fathers in 325 AD! All Inquisitions, Crusades and Holocausts have been done against the Jews in the name of Christ; both Catholic, Orthodox and Protestant have Jewish blood on their hands and have plundered all of our possessions!

Extravagant sacrificial restitution and giving is needed. Every Christian should be supporting the Messianic move in Israel among the Jews and from Israel to the nations, as Jews are called to be a light to the nations.

We Jews should not struggle to pay for our buildings and congregational halls. The whole church should be sacrificing and making restitution for the continual sins of their ancestors throughout over 1,600 years!

Any church, any area, region, city or nation that would do this, coupled with prayer and worship, would open a portal of heaven!

Curses would break, people would begin to get saved; dramatic healings would occur, prosperity would set in! Entire nations would open for revival!

Where are the contact points – the Abrahams, the Solomons and the Davids? Where are those princes and kings that would open portals of heaven and would avert judgment and bring in revival?

Accepting the Jews back is not only a greeting of *"Welcome you brother or sister."* Accepting and receiving the Messianic Jew back is to lavishly give to make restitution, establish, strengthen and support, so that these Messianic Jews would rise up and succeed! When you occupy yourself that the Jews would be prosperous and successful, Yah will occupy Himself in making you prosperous and successful!

Romans 11:15 says that "*The acceptance of the Jews is life from the dead.*" It is *revival* for your region, but how are you receiving them?

If there is no sacrificial giving, you have missed the opportunity of opening a portal of heaven and of breaking the curse of the region.

The word says that the Gentiles are debtors to the Jews because the spiritual riches came from them. How much more is the church world-wide a debtor because she has plundered the Jews in the name of Christ and rejected them for so long even when they come into her, by calling them Judaizers? This is a great sin before God. Repentance, prayer and restitution is the only key to break this;

"*For if the Gentiles have shared in their spiritual things they are indebted to minister to them also in material things*"

—Romans 15:27

The true Ecclesia is the God appointed portal of heaven!

We already know that in order to open portals of heaven, we need a contact point – a person. By far, the most meaningful contact point that the Creator has ever responded to is His own only Begotten Son, Yeshua the Messiah. Yeshua became that contact point for all times that through His worship and extravagant sacrifice would open the portal of heaven for Israel and for all nations.

In order to open the heavens before sinful mankind, *Yahveh needed a contact point*—Yeshua's unreserved sacrifice of Himself did it!

The true church/Bride became the *moving* Throne of Yah, His portal of heaven! On Shavuot, 2,000 years ago or so on the day of Pentecost, the glory of Yah sat and penetrated 120 Jews in the upper room in Jerusalem. They had laid down everything that they had; their professions and livelihoods and had come to sacrifice at the Temple, at the time of the feast and to worship and pray *until* the promise of the Father would be poured out on them! They were combining worship, prayer and sacrifice. They had left all to follow and obey the Master who had been extravagantly sacrificed for them. And as always, the portal of heaven opened up and the glory of Yah sat on them and penetrated every one of them! From that moment, that early Jewish church became the *throne of the glory of God* and they were accompanied with astounding signs, wonders and miracles and *extravagant giving* kept on accompanying the move in Jerusalem, as they had all things in common and they laid their possessions at the Apostles feet.

That young church became the portal of heaven for Israel and all the nations; wherever they went, the kingdom advanced!

When did this stop? When the Jewish roots and the Torah was rejected, and the Messianic Jews were expelled!

Since then, the church has not fully regained that position of a "portal to heaven" and throughout many generations, it was a "gate of hell," literally! How can she regain this heavenly position *fully*? By receiving the Jews and especially the Messianic and apostolic Jews and giving them a place of honor in her midst!

Receiving them with extravagant love and giving will set the pace for this end time *restoration* that is long overdue.

If the whole church would begin to pray for Israel first and give to Israel first, and especially to the Messianic end time Jewish ministers *first*, the church would begin to become a portal of heaven again; angelic visitation, signs, wonders, miracles and national-ethnic salvations would be the order of the *day*!

"In you (Abraham-Israel) all the families of the earth will be blessed – IF they bless you and honor you!" (Paraphrased from Genesis 12:3)

WHY IS EXTRAVAGANT SACRIFICE & GIVING THE KEY?

Because love is the key. Extravagant, sacrificial, unreserved giving denotes a heart of love and *love never fails!*

"For where your treasure is your heart will be also."

—Matthew 6:21

"I will love (bless) them that love (bless) you"

—Genesis 12:3

"For God so *loved* the world that He *gave* His only begotten son"

—John 3:16

Extravagant love through giving will always move God to action! Every Christian, every church, every ministry throughout the world should be looking for ways to bless/ love Israel in action, beginning with the Messianic Jews that are doing the work of the LORD in Israel and the nations. No amount of giving will be able to pay for the sins of the church concerning the Jews. Christians have plundered our lives, our homes, businesses and possessions for over 1,600 years and God has not forgotten, *since restitution has never been made!*

In order to break the spiritual drought and bring in true lasting revival, restitution needs to be made!

Not only prayers of repentance but *acts* of *giving* and *restoration*! This is THE KEY OF ABRAHAM for end time revival, and there is no other! *The blood of the Jews is crying out from the ground all over the world,* just like in 2 Samuel 21, the blood of the Gibeonites was crying out and it caused a drought in Israel for three years.

King David was not to blame, but he was suffering for the sins of Saul. This generation in the church is also suffering for the sins of past generations!

The only answer is extravagant giving, honoring and restitution. Remove the tears from the Jewish people's eyes by your extravagant love, honoring and giving; beginning with the Messianic Jews and you will experience heaven on earth!

God is calling a kingly and worshipful "David generation" into *action* through extravagant love, honor, prayer and giving into the Jewish people; beginning with the Messianic Jews and those doing the work of the LORD and instructing the church for revival. This is the way for the church, the Ecclesia to become a portal of heaven on earth again!

"And all families of the earth will be blessed."

—Genesis 12:3b

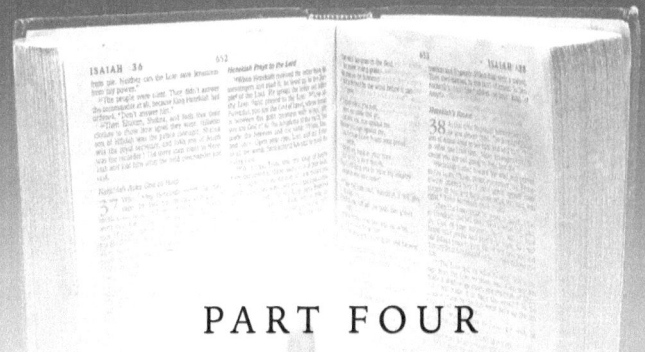

PART FOUR

RELEASING THE BLESSING OF ABRAHAM & END TIME REVIVAL

*"I will bless him that blesses you and will
curse him that lightly esteems you."*
—Genesis 12:3 paraphrased from the Hebrew

Has God brought a Jew to your life? His purpose is that this Jew will become your point of contact for the reversal of generational curses and the release of His blessings to you, to your family and to your nation!

WHAT IS A POINT OF CONTACT?

A point of contact is like an electric socket. If you are careful to put the right plug in, electricity comes out to bless your life with *light* and *power.* That electricity will warm you up when you are cold and refresh you when you are warm. It will generate power for all that you need. If you put in the wrong plug with the wrong voltage, it can burn your appliances up and it can electrocute you. If you plug in your bare fingers and do not honor the 'socket,' it can surely kill you.

Electric sockets, though dangerous if mishandled, are the source of the utmost blessings! We would find it hard to live without them in our 21st century and we tend to take them for granted. However, we should be so grateful for them, every day!

We, Jews are like that electric socket; we are the source of blessing for all mankind, for all families, tribes and nations of the Earth. The Creator said that He will bless all those that treat us well and handle us with respect; All those individuals, tribes and nations that 'plug into us' in the correct manner shall be supplied with the blessing of *light* and *power*.

"All the families of the earth will be blessed if they bless Abraham and his descendants the Jewish people."
—Genesis 12:3 Paraphrased

However, if you mishandle us, take us lightly or dishonor us, 'plugging incorrectly into us', death and destruction is released. The curse is released! For over 1600 years, the Gentile Christians have 'plugged wrongly' into us by dishonoring us, our Jewishness, the Torah and all that we represent. They have taught the nations to 'plug wrongly into us'. This has cost the life of many and it has put all nations under the curse instead of the blessing! We are in the 21st century and not one entire nation or tribe has been saved! Most of the world is in darkness! The condition is so serious that a great surge of *light* and *power* is needed in order to rescue this world. We are your point of contact in order to release this great amount of light and power, enough to bless your life, your family and your nation!*But you have to "Plug into us correctly".*

"He will bless those that bless us"

—Genesis 12:3

BIBLICAL EXAMPLES OF RIGHT 'PLUGGING' INTO THE 'JEWISH BLESSING SOCKET'

Rehab – A prostitute with no future and no hope
She fed and protected the Israeli spies, risking her life!She and her family were the only ones spared when Jericho was destroyed. She quit prostitution and married a Jew!

Later on, she is shown as being honored to the highest position as part of the Royal Lineage of King David and the Messiah Himself! (Joshua 2, 6:17, Matthew 1)

Ruth – A widow and a cursed Moabite
She became like Abraham as she left her family, her gods and her inheritance in Moab and sowed her life in its entirety to become a helper, a companion and a blessing to her penniless, widowed and grief-stricken mother in law. Ruth was making restitution for the sins of her ancestors in Moab who did not help the Jewish people when they needed it in the desert! Her act of honor towards one suffering and broken Jew reversed the curse of her ancestors and won her the favor

of God and of the richest and most influential Jew of Bethlehem. Boaz became her kinsman redeemer and her husband, and she was elevated to the highest position that a woman could have in Bethlehem of Judah. She is grafted into Israel and into the full blessing of Abraham and became part of the royal lineage of King David and of the Messiah Himself! (Deuteronomy 23:3, Ruth)

Cornelius – A God-fearing Gentile yet excluded from the covenant!

In the midst of the 'Jew hating' Roman Empire, he chose to go against the current by honoring and blessing the Jews. Cornelius was making restitution to the Jews for the way that his Roman country men mistreated them, abused them with taxes and despised them. He prayed constantly for them and gave of his substance to help them and honor them. His prayers and giving to the Jews built a Memorial before Elohim, the Creator. YAH (God) *remembered* him and saved his whole family and circle of friends! He entered into history as the *first* Gentile to enter into the covenant of Abraham, through the blood of Yeshua and without the need of physical circumcision. He is the father of all Gentile believers! May all of them begin to follow his Godly example in making restitution through giving, praying and honoring of the Jews that have been dishonored, mistreated and plundered in the name of Christ, by Gentile Christians throughout a painfully bloody history! (Acts 10).

As Yah (God) connected you with us as end time apostolic Jews, we are your point of contact! As we have come to your nation, we have become your point of contact. Light, power, miracles, healing and the blessing of Abraham is available to you *if* you 'plug in properly' like Rehab, Ruth and Cornelius!

"Faith touching" and honoring us to receive instruction from us releases the miracles as in the case of the woman with the issue of blood. Many were pressing on to Yeshua but only *one* touched Him to the point that virtue came out to heal her impossible condition! She did not care what anyone would say – she pushed herself through the discouraging crowds; she honored Him as the Messiah; she believed in His ability to heal her, and when she touched Him in the right way, virtue came out. Those that touch us in the right way and honor us to instruct them according to Zachariah 8:23 will go with us and be healed and restored and will *become restorers themselves.* The hem/fringes/*tsitsit* of the garment represent the Torah and the commandments! Greatness is promised to those who follow us as we teach them. (Numbers 15: 38, 39 Matthew 5:17-20, Malachi 4:4-6)

Sacrificial and ultra-generous faith giving to us releases the protection, favor, blessing and family salvation and restoration that seemed unattainable to you. We are your Jewish contact point.

Just like in the electric socket, what is really important is the electricity that is released from it, yet without the socket,

There is no *outlet* and the electricity cannot flow. So, it is with us Jews, what is really important is the God-given light (word) and power (Spirit) that flow through us, but without us 'Jewish sockets' and 'contact points,' there is no *outlet* for the blessing! Romans 11:18 says *"Do not be arrogant against the (Jewish Sockets) branches, but if you are remember that you do not support the Root but the Root supports you."*

We are your Jewish point of contact for the reversal of generational curses, for your healing and miracles, for the blessing of Abraham to be released on you, your family and your nations. Plug in today! Let your faith giving like Cornelius, Rehab and Ruth release the fullness of Yah's favor in your life! Let the miracles flow*!* However, *remember* that Rehab, Ruth and Cornelius *loved* and *honored* the Jewish people. They acted upon that love and honor and it released the blessings! The Jews are the spiritual parents of all believing Gentiles! (Romans 15:27)

"And now abides faith, hope and love, but the greatest of these is *love.*"

—1 Corinthians 13:13

We can paraphrase Genesis 12:3 as follows;

"I, the Creator will love those who love you Abraham and your Jewish children and they express it in word, thought and deed; and I will hate those that do not appreciate and honor them. And in you, as they love you and your Jewish children, all the tribes, families and nations of the earth will experience My love and I will redeem them!"

And love never fails! True love gives the best she has!

We go through many nations, but only those that 'plug in' in faith through love, only those that give their best and continue to do so, keep the light and the power on! Those that 'enjoy' our coming but do not plug in, miss a great opportunity to enter into an unstoppable blessing and end time revival. For 1,600 years, the church has been plugging wrongly by persecuting, hating, rejecting and killing Jews; thus, releasing the curse instead of the blessing. You are invited to *reverse* all that!

You know how. Your right plugging into us will not only bless your life and save your family but will actually begin to release light and power into your dark and deserted region. Because of you, your nation can be blessed and saved!

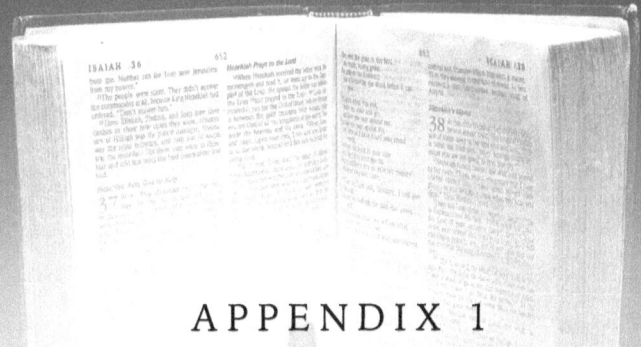

A BRIEF HISTORICAL RECOUNT

The reason Jewish roots were lost early in Church history is that our revered Church fathers were anti-Semitic, deliberately changing Jewish celebrations and altering some doctrines to make a complete break from Judaism. In the second century, Justin Martyr, Polycarp, and Marcion were among those beginning the onslaught against the Jewish people and Judaism. Marcion in the middle of the second century was the first to write that the New Covenant had replaced all previous covenants -- and he was known as a heretic. His writing was later taken seriously and led to replacement theology, the elements of which show up in the Thompson Chain Reference Bible. On the back of the New Testament title page, there is a chart listing contrasts between the Old and New Testaments, including spiritual darkness vs. light of the world, death reigns vs. life eternal and fifteen others. Jesus and His disciples would not agree with that chart.

Jesus said, *"Do not think that I came to abolish the Torah...* (Matthew 5:17-20)

In the fourth century, John Chrysostom, known for powerful, eloquent sermons, gave a series of seventeen virulently anti-Semitic sermons at a time when the Pagan celebration of Ishtar (Easter), the fertility goddess, was set to replace Passover for the celebration of Jesus' death and resurrection. Also, the Roman winter solstice celebration in honor of the god Saturn was established as the celebration of Jesus' birth. In the fifth century, Augustine brought Greek philosophy into Christian theology, which have influenced the church to this day.

The celebrations introduced in the fourth century put a seal on the separation from Judaism and set the stage for violence against the Jewish people. Jewish people even today often view Christians as "The enemy" but with good reason. Over the centuries, Christians have outperformed all other groups combined in the killing of Jews. There were numerous pogroms throughout Europe from early on through the Holocaust. In medieval Spain, children at the age of eight were taken from Jewish parents to be raised in Christian homes. Jews were frequently forced to convert to Christianity, and then afterward, were still persecuted for having been Jewish. In 1492, Ferdinand and Isabella forced all the Jews to leave

Spain. Such forced exoduses were common, with Jews moving from one country to another, virtually all over Europe. Every European country expelled Jews at least once. Jews were forbidden to own land until they came to the American colonies. The Spanish Inquisition is well known for cruelty to the Jewish people.

The Holocaust was not the end of anti-Semitism and not the sole evidence of it in WW II. During the Holocaust, not one Christian denomination spoke out against the attempted extermination of the Jewish people. The US government turned away a ship loaded with Jewish refugees from Europe and forced it to return to Europe to certain death for the passengers. US bombers flew over Auschwitz nearly every night to bomb railroad marshalling yards just a few miles away, but never bombed the gas chambers, seemingly to "avoid possible collateral damage, killing or injuring prisoners" who were going to be gassed in the very near future. Today, Anti-Semitism is rising throughout the world, especially in Europe. It is very strong at the UN.

To understand the Jewish roots of Christianity, look first to the Hebrew scriptures. Among the first things that the early church did to divorce from Judaism was changing the seasons of the LORD. These are detailed in Leviticus 23, beginning with the Sabbath.

The church at Constantine's behest, moved Jesus' death and resurrection from Passover and introduced Easter, then added Christmas to celebrate Jesus' birth. His birth, death, and resurrection certainly need to be honored, but not with pagan holidays. As the church returns to its Jewish roots, it is not to copy modern Judaism, to be pretend Jews. The church needs to study scripture, honoring the commandments that have been forsaken, becoming "worshipers in Spirit and in truth." (Reverend Bill Moreford, *The Seasons of the* LORD)

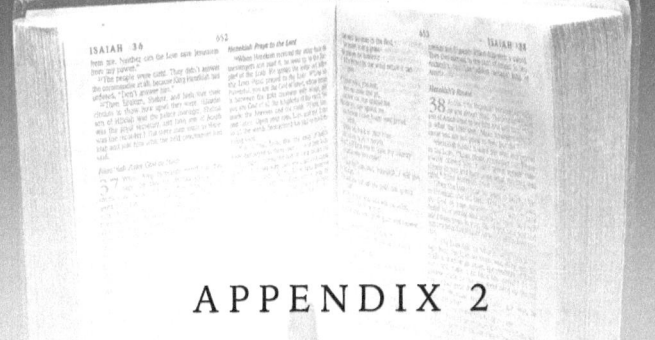

APPENDIX 2
TWO WEDDINGS & ONE DIVORCE

THE FIRST MARRIAGE

The following illustration will explain why Christianity was 'the womb' of the Spanish Inquisition, the Crusades, and the Nazi Holocaust. Yahveh-God is looking to the church for repentance in order to influence the nations and fulfill the mandate of Matthew 28:19 *"Go and make disciples of all nations."*

The first and original church was married to a Jewish Husband by the name of Yeshua the Messiah & into His family the Jewish people (Ephesians 2:14 and Romans 11). The Wedding Ceremony took place in Jerusalem. It was ratified and sealed by the spilling of the blood of the Husband and by the breaking of His body. (Luke 22:15–20) The time of this marriage was the holy biblical Feast of Passover. The fruit of this miraculous wedding was thousands and thousands of people, both Jews and Gentiles, saved and healed. Even the shadow of this holy bride healed the sick, as signs and wonders and miracles followed her wherever she went in the name of her Husband Yeshua.

This marriage led the wife to much suffering. Many in the world did not love her Husband and tried to kill her by persecuting her and even throwing her to the lions during the Roman Empire's reign of terror. Those were hard years. After many years of suffering, Yeshua's wife had become weary. He had gone to prepare a place for her and had not come back yet.

She started to get tired from her lifestyle as an outcast, persecuted and hunted at every corner. She longed for peace at any price. She longed for the warm embrace of a Husband who would provide her with peace and security here on this earth... At her weakest point an earthly king appeared. (Matthew 10:34, John 14:27, Jeremiah 8:11)

This earthly king was influential and powerful by earthly standards. He could stop the killing and persecution against her. He could give her the security she longed for... *If* only she would agree to divorce this Jewish Husband of hers and completely separate from His family Israel, and from that Book that she treasured so much – where He had left her all of His instructions and the family legacy of God's Word.

This powerful king seemed to be a spiritual man. He claimed that her Jewish Husband had appeared to him in a dream and had given him the crown of the Roman Empire. His deceptive charm and appeasing manners managed to attract the very weary bride of Messiah, but not all were deceived. There was a portion of the bride/church/ecclesia that was not fooled by the charms of this deceitful king. These were the Messianic Jews of the time.

They were too rooted in the writings of the Holy Book and the ancient Hebrew Scriptures to be deceived. But the vast majority of the believers at that time were Gentiles, and they did not want any more suffering on behalf of the Book, its Author, or His family.

They wanted freedom and peace at all cost.

The powerful Constantine sang the song of peace and safety and prepared a bed of roses... The Gentile portion of the church slept with him, falling into violent adultery and wounding the heart of her heavenly Jewish Husband. In order to appease the conscience of this adulterous church, Constantine decided to legalize this unholy union in the year AD 325 by means of a wedding ceremony called the Council of Nicaea and drawing up an ungodly and illegal marriage contract called the Nicean Creed.

He used his worldly power to draw all the gentile church fathers, which for the most part were already anti-Semitic and hated their Jewish roots. These church fathers were to be witnesses of this horrendous divorce and the adulterous new marriage between the predominantly Gentile church and another Jesus, a product of Constantine's own creation.

This alternative Savior came with another family, another book (totally disconnected from the ancient Hebrew writings), other customs, Laws, festivals, traditions and ways of measuring time.

Knowing that his brand-new wife was accustomed to worshipping God, he organized for her a god that would suit her perfectly by not demanding any holiness from her. He presented a god of peace that was lenient towards a mixture of paganism and holiness: An all-inclusive god, who accepted all traditions and blended them into one.

Now Passover and First Fruits, the festival of Yeshua's resurrection, would become The Feast of Ishtar, the goddess of fertility, or Easter with bunny rabbits and Easter eggs. (At that time eggs were dipped in the blood of the babies sacrificed to the goddess, thus the tradition of painting the eggs).

Now the fay of worship would change from Shabbat to Sunday in order to eternalize the sun god who for now would be called Jesus – yet it was another Jesus and certainly not Yeshua, the Jewish Messiah.

Then the day of the winter solstice of witchcraft, called Saturnalia or Paganalia, celebrated on the 25th of December in the Roman Empire, was to acquire the name Christmas and would celebrate the birth of this false Messiah. For the true Messiah was born during the holy biblical Feast of Tabernacles and followed the Hebrew biblical calendar, not the Roman one. (Daniel 7:25–27, Jeremiah 10:2–4 about the Christmas tree.)

The ancient Holy Book of the Hebrew Scriptures was to become obsolete, and its Laws done away with. Instead, Constantine compiled the apostolic writings, the letters of Paul and others into a new holy book and called it the New Testament. He gave this holy book his own perverse interpretation, completely divorced from the foundational

Hebrew Writings whom he and his followers called the 'Old Testament.' (Matthew 5:17–21)

> "In rejecting their custom, we may transmit to our descendants the legitimate way of celebrating Easter... We ought not therefore to have anything in common with the Jew, for the Savior has shown us another way; our worship following a more legitimate and more convenient course (the order of the days of the week); And consequently, in unanimously adopting this mode, we desire dearest brethren to separate ourselves from the detestable company of the Jew." (Excerpt from *The Nicene Creed*, year 325, found in *Eusebius, Vita Const. Lib III 18-20)*

This creed and its instructions are still followed by most Christians today with the celebration of Easter, Christmas, Sunday (replacing Shabbat), and the rejection of the Laws of God.

Indeed, a new religion had been born. It had a gentile god by the name of Jesus Christ, an apostle by the name of Constantine, a new book by the name of the New Testament (although compiled from the apostolic writings, which are completely Yah-inspired, it was deceitfully interpreted through gentile eyes and gentile theologians), and new traditions, and unholy festivals such as Easter, Christmas, Sunday, and Halloween.

And most importantly... *no Jews*... no, not even the Messiah.

What has been the fruit of this adulterous marriage?

Either make the tree good and its fruit good, or else make the tree bad and its fruit bad; for a tree is known by its fruit.

Matthew 12:33

The fruit of the first holy matrimony were salvations and healings. The fruit of this ungodly and pagan marriage were forced conversions and killings, yes even mass destructions of the family of Yeshua the Messiah, (the true Husband), in the name of the false Jesus Christ god created by Constantine.

A god who, according to Constantine in the Nicene Creed, had shown us *another way*. What was that way? It is a way of jealousy, hatred, killing, destruction, and Lawlessness. Horrendous Christian events such as pogroms, the holy inquisition, and the holocaust, have taken place since this ungodly 4th century marriage and the creation of this false religion.

The hatred conveyed in the Nicene Creed against the Jews and anything Jewish, including the Torah and the Old Testament, has continued through the great Protestant Reformation of the 16th century, and it still influences Christians today.

The following excerpt is from *Our Hands are Stained with Blood* by Michael Brown, as he quotes directly from Martin Luther's writings.

Luther wrote this after he was frustrated from trying to evangelize the Jews and when he was old and sick:

> "What shall we Christians do with this damned rejected race of Jews? First, their synagogues should be set on fire. Secondly, their homes should likewise be broken down and destroyed. Thirdly, they should be deprived of their prayer books and Talmud's. Fourthly, their rabbis must be forbidden under threat of death to teach anymore. Fifthly, passports and traveling privileges should be absolutely forbidden to the Jews... To sum up dear princes and nobles, who have Jews in your domains, if this advice of mine does not suit you, then find a better one. So that you and we may all be free of this insufferable, devilish burden – the Jews." (Luther and Brown)

Hitler followed Luther's instructions meticulously and quoted him while doing so. The fruit? Over six million Jews exterminated in horrendous death camps and gas chambers, and many survivors scarred for life.

PROPHETIC ALTAR CALL

After two days He will revive us; on the third day He will raise us up, that we may live in His sight. Let us know; let us pursue the knowledge of Yahveh. His going forth is established as the morning; He will come to us like the rain, like the latter and former rain to the earth.

Hosea 6:2–3

The Third Day is upon us, the Third Millennium, and this is the Father's call to His Third Day church:

Come let us return to Yeshua, to our Jewish Messiah, His Jewish family and His ancient Hebrew Scriptures. Come let us reinterpret the New Testament through the eyes of the holy Scriptures. Let us separate ourselves from our pagan husband, Constantine, and his false Jesus and let us go back to the true Messiah Yeshua, to His Father's Laws and Precepts, to true divine holy grace, to true love and holiness. Let us return to Jerusalem, and let us be made whole from centuries of adultery and paganism, as we go back to the original apostolic Jewish roots of our faith.

In Yeshua's love and brokenness;

Archbishop Dr. Dominiquae & Rabbi Baruch Bierman

Disclaimer: What this Article is Not Saying

- It is *not* saying to go back to the laws of Rabbinic Judaism.
- It is *not* implying that all Christians have anti-Semitism.
- It is *not* disqualifying the countless believers who call on the name of Jesus Christ meaning the *true* Jewish Messiah Yeshua.

- It is *not* disqualifying worship on Sunday, Monday, Tuesday or any other day.
- It is *not* disqualifying the New Testament as Bible (Only the wrong, 'divorced' interpretations of it).

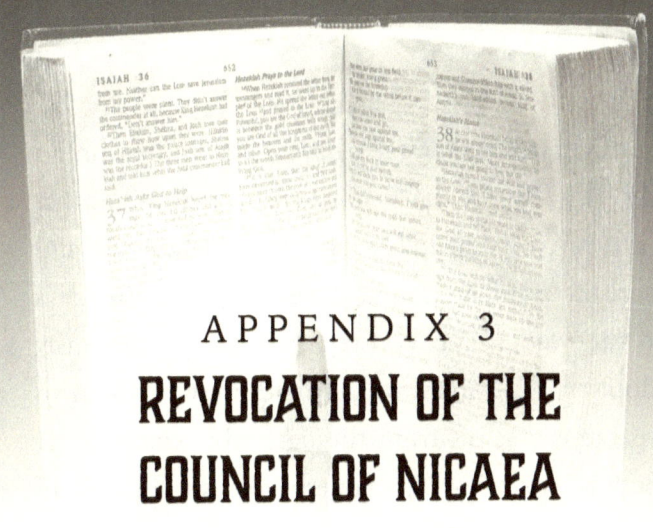

APPENDIX 3

REVOCATION OF THE COUNCIL OF NICAEA

From the letter of the Emperor (Constantine) to all those not present at the council. (Found in Eusebius, Vita Const.,Lib III 18-20)

When the question relative to the sacred festival of Easter arose, it was universally thought that it would be convenient that all should keep the feast on one day; for what could be more beautiful and more desirable than to see this festival, through which we receive the hope of immortality, celebrated by all with one accord and in the same manner? It was declared to be particularly unworthy for this, the holiest of festivals, to follow the customs (the calculation) of the Jews who had soiled their hands with the most fearful of crimes, and whose minds were blinded. In rejecting their custom we may transmit to our descendants the legitimate mode of celebrating Easter; which we have observed from the time of the Saviour's passion (according to the day of the week).

We ought not, therefore, to have anything in common with the Jew, for the Saviour has shown us another way; our worship following a more legitimate and more convenient course (the order of the days of the week: And consequently in unanimously adopting this mode, we desire, dearest brethren to separate ourselves from the detestable company of the Jew. For it is truly shameful for us to hear them boast that without their direction, we could not keep this feast. How can they be in the right, they who, after the death of the Saviour, have no longer been led by reason but by wild violence, as their delusion may urge them? They do not possess the truth in this Easter question, for in their blindness and repugnance to all improvements they frequently celebrate two Passovers in the same year. We could not imitate those who are openly in error.

How, then, could we follow these Jews who are most certainly blinded by error? For to celebrate a Passover twice in one year, is totally inadmissible.

But even if this were not so it would still be your duty not to tarnish your soul by communication with such wicked people (the Jews). You should consider not only that the number of churches in these provinces make a majority, but also that it is right to demand what our reason approves, and that we should have nothing in common with the Jews.

(Gleaned from Dr. Henry R. Percival's *"The Nicaean and Post Nicaean Fathers."* Vol. XIV Grand Rapid: Erdmans pub. 1979, pgs. 54-55)

EXPOSING THE 23 LIES & DOCTRINAL ERRORS

1. "When the question relative to the sacred festival of Easter..."

The truth: sacred to pagan traditions, this is a pagan name derived from the goddess Ishtar. (Exodus 20:3, Hosea 2:17)

2. "...arose, it was universally..."

The truth: Everyone in the universe? Is Constantine the king of the universe? (Isaiah 14:3)

3. "...thought that it would be convenient..."

The truth: God does not call us to convenience but obedience. (John 15:10)

4. "...that all should keep the feast on one day; for what could be more beautiful and more desirable than to see this festival, through which we receive the hope of immortality, celebrated by all with one accord and in the same manner?...."

The truth: Without Jews? John 17:21, unity between Jew and Gentile brings the salvation of all mankind. (Psalms 133 and Isaiah 56)

5. "...It was declared to be particularly unworthy..."

The truth: Yahveh's choice of dates is "unworthy" to Constantine as he sets himself above God's choosing of timings. (Daniel 7:25 and Isaiah 14:13 [Lucifer])

6. "...for this, the holiest of festivals to follow the customs (the calculation) of the Jews..."

The truth: Which are the original and true calculations? (Leviticus 23:1, Jeremiah 31:31–34)

7. "...who had soiled their hands with the most fearful of crimes, and whose minds were blinded..."

The truth: In John 10:17–18 Yeshua lays His own life down (See also John 3:16.) the accusation that "The Jews killed Christ" has been the incentive for the extermination of millions of Jews from that point onwards and until this day, including the Holocaust. (See Matthew 7:17–20, the fruit of this theology)

8. "...In rejecting their custom..."

The truth: God's custom according to His Word.

9. "...we may transmit to our descendants the legitimate..."

The truth: according to Constantine but not according to the Word of God. (Matthew 26:2, Leviticus 23:1–4, Genesis 1:14, John 20:1–9, Matthew 12:39)

10. "...mode of celebrating Easter which we have observed..."

The truth: pagan name and feast not mentioned in the Holy Scriptures.

11. "We ought not therefore to have anything in common with the Jew, for the Savior has shown us another way"

The truth: Yeshua is Jewish, so if nothing is in common with the Jews, nothing is in common with the Messiah. (Matthew 1, John 19;19, Luke 1:59, Luke 2:21)

12. "our worship following a more legitimate and more convenient course, the order of the days of the week"

The truth: Constantine legitimizes his own ideas in order to gain political power and control and he attempts to dethrone the Word of God on this subject – setting himself and his opinions above Yah and His unchanging Word.

13. "...And consequently in unanimously..."

The truth: without the Jews from which salvation comes! (John 4:22)

14. "...adopting this mode, we desire, dearest brethren to separate ourselves from the detestable company of the Jew For it is truly shameful for us to hear them boast that without their direction we could not keep this feast. How can they be in the right, they who, after the death of the Savior..."

The truth: Romans 11:15–20 warns the Gentiles not to be arrogant against the Jews or Gentiles will be cut of the Olive tree!

15. "...have no longer been led by reason..."

The truth: True sons of God are not led by reason or Greek philosophy but by the Spirit of God. Since Constantine and the Council of Nicaea, the church in its vast majority has been led by reason and by theologians instead of by powerful apostles. (Romans 8:14, Ephesians 2:20) - these are all Jewish.

16. "but by wild violence, as their delusion may urge them"

The truth: What wild violence is he talking about? Unsupported accusation used many times to incite the masses against the Jews like in the Protocols of the Elders of Zion?

17. "They do not possess the truth in this Easter question, for in their blindness and [15th lie] repugnance to all improvements"

The truth: traditions of demons and men that make null and void the Word of God (Matthew 15:3,4, Mark 7:13)

18. "They frequently celebrate two Passovers in the same year. We could not imitate those who are openly in error. How, then, could we follow these Jews who are most certainly blinded by error?"

The truth: Is following the biblical customs error? Who is really blinded here? Gentiles are supposed to be grafted into Israel's Olive tree and not vice versa! (Romans 11:15–20)

19. "For to celebrate a Passover twice in one year is totally inadmissible."

The truth: 2 Chronicles 30:1–3, it is totally scriptural.

20. "But even if this were not so it would still be your duty not to tarnish your soul by communication with such wicked people (the Jews)."

The truth: In other words, Constantine's purpose is to separate from the Jews and the Torah no matter what! Why? 1 John 4:1–3 states that the spirit of anti-Messiah, in operation through Constantine, removes the identity of Messiah as a Jew, and sets himself above God and His Word and His sovereign choice of choosing the Jews to bring salvation.

21. "You should consider not only that the number of churches in these provinces make a majority"

The truth: God has never worked with "majorities" but with obedience. Trusting in the arm of the flesh or the opinions of men brings about a curse! (Deuteronomy 28:1–14, Jeremiah 17:5, Judges 7:2–8, 1 Samuel 14:6)

22. "...but also that it is right to demand what our reason approves..."

The truth: Human reasoning? (1 Corinthians 1:27, Isaiah 29:14b)

23. "...and that we should have nothing in common with the Jews."

The truth: or with the Jewish Messiah or His salvation – John 4:22, Romans 11:15–20. He set the Gentile part of the church onto a path of self-destruction, remaining a wild olive instead of being grafted into the cultivated Olive tree – which is Israel – because of arrogance, removing the foundations of the Jewish apostles and prophets. (Psalms 11:3, Ephesians 2:20, Revelation 21:14)

PRAYER RENOUNCING THE FIRST COUNCIL OF NICAEA

Please pray. You can copy and pass it on, and please let us know of your decision.

Before the Almighty God of Israel, I stand and

hereby renounce the First Council of Nicaea as led by Constantine. I renounce its foundation and all the anti-Jewish fruit that came out of it. I renounce every doctrinal error and every lie in it, including replacement theology in all of its aspects.

I hereby affirm my faith in Yahveh, the God of Israel, who is the Creator of the Universe and my Father through the atoning death of His Holy Son Yeshua, who is both the promised Jewish Messiah and God in the flesh. I hereby affirm my faith in the resurrection of Yeshua the Messiah and the outpouring of the Holy Spirit of God from the Day of Shavuot (Pentecost) and onwards, to all that repent and believe in the Son. I hereby affirm my belief that I am grafted into the Olive Tree that represents Israel, and together with the believing Jewish people, I will inherit eternal life. I hereby affirm that the God of Israel will never forsake His people, neither will He forget His covenant with the Jews or with the Ecclesia (Called out Ones - Church).

I thank you, Holy Father, for removing all the curses that have come into my life and into my nation due to our belief in the tenets of faith stated in the Council of Nicaea concerning the Jews and the Jewish foundations of the faith. I beg you and thank you for pouring out your great mercy and forgiveness over myself, my family, and my nation. I hereby commit myself to walk in truth as You reveal it to me and in love with all my fellow men and especially my (and the Church's) spiritual parents, the Jewish people, according to Genesis 12:1-3.

APPENDIX 4
CONNECT WITH US

OTHER BOOKS
Order now online: www.kad-esh.org/shop/

The MAP Revolution (Free E-Book)
Find Out Why Revival Does Not Come... Yet!

The Identity Theft
The Return of the 1st Century Messiah

From Sickology to a Healthy Logic
The Product of 18 Years Walking Through Psychiatric
Hospitals

ATG: Addicts Turning to God
The Biblical Way to Handle Addicts and Addictions

The Healing Power of the Roots
It's a Matter of Life or Death!

Grafted In
It's Time to Take the Nation's!

Sheep Nations
It's Time to Take the Nations!

Restoring the Glory: The Original Way
The Ancient Paths Rediscovered

Stormy Weather
Judgment Has Already Begun, Revival is Knocking at the
Door

Yeshua is the Name
The Important Restoration of the Original
Hebrew Name of the Messiah

Defeating Depression
This Book is a Kiss from Heaven!

Let's Get Healthy, Saints!
The Biblical Guide to Nutrition

Yes!
The Dramatic Salvation of
Archbishop Dr. Dominiquae Bierman

Eradicating the Cancer of Religion
Hint: All People Have It

Restoration of Holy Giving
Releasing the True 1,000 Fold Blessing

Vision Negev
The Awesome Restoration of the Sephardic Jews

The Woman Factor by Rabbi Baruch Bierman
Freedom From Womanphobia

The Revival of the Third Day (Free E-Book)
The Return to Yeshua the Jewish Messiah

Music Albums

www.kad-esh.org/shop/

The Key of Abraham

Abba Shebashamayim

Uru

Retorno

Get Equipped & Partner with Us

Global Revival MAP (GRM) Israeli Bible School
Take the most comprehensive video Bible school online that
focuses on dismantling replacement theology.
For more information or to order, please contact us:

www.grmbibleschool.com
grm@dominiquaebierman.com

United Nations for Israel Movement

We invite you to join us as a member and partner with $25
a month, which supports the advancing of this End time
vision that will bring true unity to the body of the Messiah.
We will see the One New Man form, witness the restoration
of Israel, and take part in the birthing of SHEEP NATIONS.
Today is an exciting time to be serving Him!

www.unitednationsforisrael.org
info@unitednationsforisrael.org

Global Re-Education Initiative (GRI)
Against Anti-Semitism

Discover the Jewishness of the Messiah and defeat Christian
anti-Semitism with this online video course to see revival in
your nation!

www.against-antisemitism.com
info@against-antisemitism.com

Join Our Annual Israel Tours

Travel through the Holy Land and watch the Hebrew Holy
Scriptures come alive.

www.kad-esh.org/tours-and-events/

To Send Offerings to Support our Work

Your help keeps this mission of restoration
going far and wide.

www.kad-esh.org/donations

CONTACT US

Archbishop Dr. Dominiquae & Rabbi Baruch Bierman

Kad-Esh MAP Ministries | www.kad-esh.org

info@kad-esh.org

United Nations for Israel | www.unitednationsforisrael.org

info@unitednationsforisrael.org

Zion's Gospel Press | shalom@zionsgospel.com

52 Tuscan Way, Ste 202-412, 32092 St. Augustine Florida, USA

+1-972-301-7087